AaBbCcDdEeFfGgHhIiJjKkLlMmNnOoPpQqRrSsTtUuVvWwXxYyZz

Quick and Creative Literature Response Activities

More Than 60 Sensational Hands-On Ideas from A to Z

By Jane Fowler and Stephanie Newlon

SCHOLASTIC
PROFESSIONAL BOOKS

NEW YORK • TORONTO • LONDON • AUCKLAND • SYDNEY

DEDICATION

This book is dedicated to the unsung heroes who labor with love in their classrooms daily. Continue to enjoy the children whose hearts and minds have been entrusted to you. Teachers really do make a difference!

ACKNOWLEDGMENTS

This book would not have been possible without the guidance of the One who cares for us all. We have been so blessed!

We must give thanks to our families who have encouraged us and allowed us time away from our responsibilities as wives and mothers in order to create and develop this labor of love. We love you!

We must also acknowledge the many students who have passed through our classrooms and taught us so much. Thanks also to the many teachers who have supported and encouraged us through our years of teaching and writing.

Interior design by Solutions by Design, Inc.
Cover design by Vincent Ceci and Jaime Lucero
Cover illustration by Teresa Anderko
Interior illustration by Ellen Sasaki
Photographs by Jane Fowler and Stephanie Newlon

ISBN 0-590-59926-7

12 11 10 9 8 7 6 5 4 3 2 1   4 5/9

TABLE OF CONTENTS

INTRODUCTION

The enjoyment of a good book can be further enhanced through the use of activities that extend learning. Most of the activities we suggest can be used with almost any book you may have on your bookshelf. We've found in our classrooms that activities such as these build a love and appreciation for literature while making teaching and learning more enjoyable for all.

How to Use the Book

Using this book is as simple as can be,
Just pick an activity from A to Z.
After reading a story, choose one to do,
In a small group, individually, or with you.
Strengthen students' comprehension, review a character's role,
Notice the setting or the problems as the story is retold.
Creating triaramas, sharing a story belt with a friend,
Making masks, graphs, and apple pies, the fun will never end.
Don't forget the family, there's a home connection too,
Suggested literature strategies that the whole family can do.
It really is that easy, pick an activity from A to Z,
The enjoyment of reading is the end product you will see.

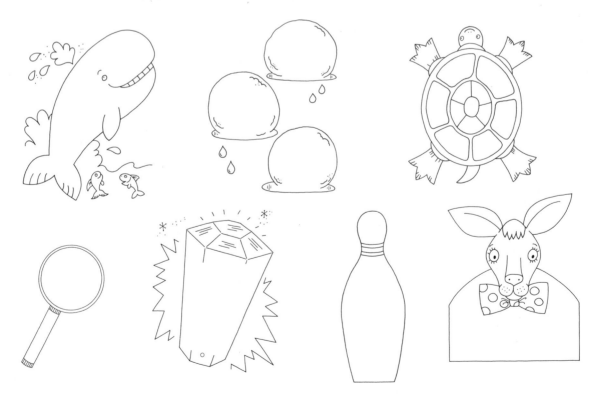

AaBbCcDdEeFfGgHhIiJjKkLlMmNnOoPpQqRrSsTtUuVvWwXxYyZz

Apple Pies

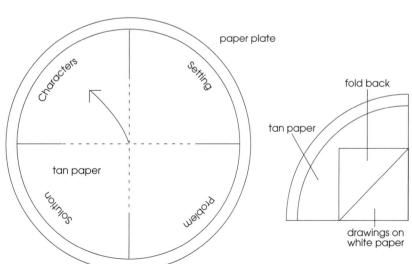

Celebrate an enjoyable book with the making of a paper "apple pie" that tells about the book. Provide each child with sheets of white and tan construction paper and a 7-inch paper plate. Have them cut a 6-inch circle from the white construction paper and a 6-inch circle from the tan construction paper. Show students how to fold both circles into fourths. Help them to cut the tan circle from the center point down each of the four fold lines to within one inch of the outside of the circle. (See the diagram.)

Invite your students to draw four story elements of your choice (for example, main characters, setting, problem, solution, etc.) inside each section of the white circle and then glue the circle onto the paper plate. Then students glue the edges of the tan circle onto the plate, being careful to keep the sections of both circles aligned. Have students label the sections on the tan circle with the names of the story elements. Your students can top off each story pie with some clear crystal glitter to look like sugar for an appealing dessert.

Children will enjoy sharing their pies as they peel back the crust to reveal the story elements drawn inside. Serve warm with laughter!

paper plate

Characters

Setting

tan paper

Solution

Problem

fold back

tan paper

drawings on white paper

Art Logs

A book's illustrations are a wonderful springboard for students to create their own artwork and "art logs." Students' art logs can be made by stapling together several 4" x 6" pieces of paper. You may also wish to create one large class art log using chart paper. After reading a book aloud to your class, call attention to the illustrations and any art elements you wish to explore.

Discuss any related vocabulary to explain the art elements. Vocabulary may be displayed on large charts. Then encourage your students to copy the vocabulary into their "art logs."

Provide art materials to enable the students to complete their own piece of art that reflects the art element taught as well as the art found in the book. Encourage students to write about their piece of art using the vocabulary in their art logs. Share and display students' work.

All About . . .

After reading a book about friendship, invite children to work in cooperative groups of four to six. One child is selected to be the subject of the poem. Each of the other children is responsible for writing one sentence that describes his or her friend. You may wish to use the poetry frame on page 7. These poems can be shared with the class when completed.

(Aa) Name Kate

All About . . .

All About Sam .

Sam is six years old.

Sam feels happy when he plays soccer.

Sam 's favorite color is purple.

Sam likes to eat pizza .

Sam is best at drawing .

Sam is my friend.

AaBbCcDdEeFfGgHhIiJjKkLlMmNnOoPpQqRrSsTtUuVvWwXxYyZz

School-Home CONNECTION

Encourage families to use the poetry frame "All About My Family" on page 8 to write a poem about themselves.

All About . . .

All About _____.

_____ is _____ years old.

_____ feels happy when _____

_____ .

_____'s favorite color is _____ .

_____ likes to eat _____ .

_____ is best at _____ .

_____ is my friend.

AaBbCcDdEeFfGgHhIiJjKkLlMmNnOoPpQqRrSsTtUuVvWwXxYyZz

Name _____

Dear Parents,

Please work together to complete the poetry frame on this page. Your child did a similar activity at school using a poetry frame to write a poem about a friend. Please return the completed poetry frame to school by _____. These poems will be shared in class.

All About My Family

My family likes to _____.

My family feels happy when _____

_____.

My family likes to eat _____.

My family plays _____.

My family is special!

AaBbCcDdEeFfGgHhIiJjKkLlMmNnOoPpQqRrSsTtUuVvWwXxYyZz

8

Binoculars

Have your students make binoculars using two empty toilet tissue rolls. The rolls can be covered with black construction paper or painted black to simulate real binoculars. Have children glue the rolls together and attach a length of black yarn for a neck strap.

Provide children with two white paper circles a bit larger than the diameter of the rolls on which to draw a scene from a favorite story. Have them glue the circles to the end of each roll on one side only.

Some children may wish to write a description of their pictures that can be rolled up and stored in the open ends of the binocular.

Have fun sharing and enjoying the scenery.

Bumper Stickers

Your students can create a bumper sticker slogan which captures the essence of a story you've read. Each five- to eight-word slogan can be written on a 4" x 12" piece of white paper. For example, from the story, *The Little Engine That Could*, a slogan could read "Just Think It and You Can Do It." These bumper stickers can be decorated with symbols from the story and finished with a colorful border. Display them on a bulletin board for the entire class to share.

Bags for Storytelling

White lunch bags and 3" x 5" index cards may be used to create storytelling bags to help students retell a favorite story. The children draw the scenes of the story on the bag. On the index cards they can draw the main characters. If you wish, they may cut out the characters and glue them onto craft sticks. Children act out the story by moving the main characters in front of the open standing bag. The characters may be dropped into the bag for easy transport to another table or classroom.

AaBbCcDdEeFfGgHhIiJjKkLlMmNnOoPpQqRrSsTtUuVvWwXxYyZz

Bowl Me Over

This literature strategy might be right up your alley. Duplicate the outline of the bowling pin provided on page 11. After reading a story, divide the class into groups of five. Distribute the bowling pins accordingly. Assign each group one of the following five categories: Main Characters, Setting, Problem, Solution, and Predictions. As an alternative you may wish to assign each person in a group one of the categories. Students should either draw or draw and write about the assigned story elements on the bowling pins. Upon completion, the members of each group will come to the front of the room and line up in order to share what they have done. The class will try to "bowl them over" with questions about their story element.

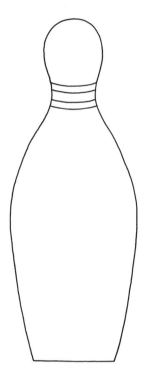

School-Home CONNECTION

Provide each student with a white bag and four index cards. Encourage families to illustrate where they live on the outside of the bag. On the index cards they can draw things that are important to them such as a family pet, favorite sport, hobby, or food.

Bowl Me Over

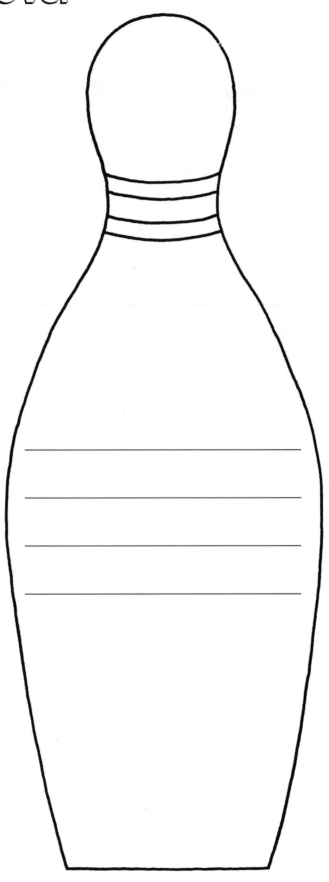

Cc

Cubes

Cubes are a fun way to help children think about a story. Children can draw their favorite characters on the cube, make a story map, or tell about a favorite character. You can also have

them use the cube to list words that have the same sounds or to write vocabulary words and their meanings. Provide children with the reproducible cube on page 13. Have them draw and write on the cubes before you demonstrate how to cut and fold them.

Clusters

Clusters are an excellent graphic organizer to use after reading any piece of literature. Clusters can be organized in several different ways. The spider web is the most common kind of cluster. The main idea is written in the middle, and supporting details spin off from the center. An extension to a class generated word bank may involve clustering the words according to subtopics, same sounds, or by the number of syllables found in each word.

School-Home CONNECTION

Provide a copy of the reproducible of the cube for each child to take home. Families may illustrate each side of the cube with a family portrait, their home, or favorite family activities. Assembled cubes can be shared and displayed at school.

Cube

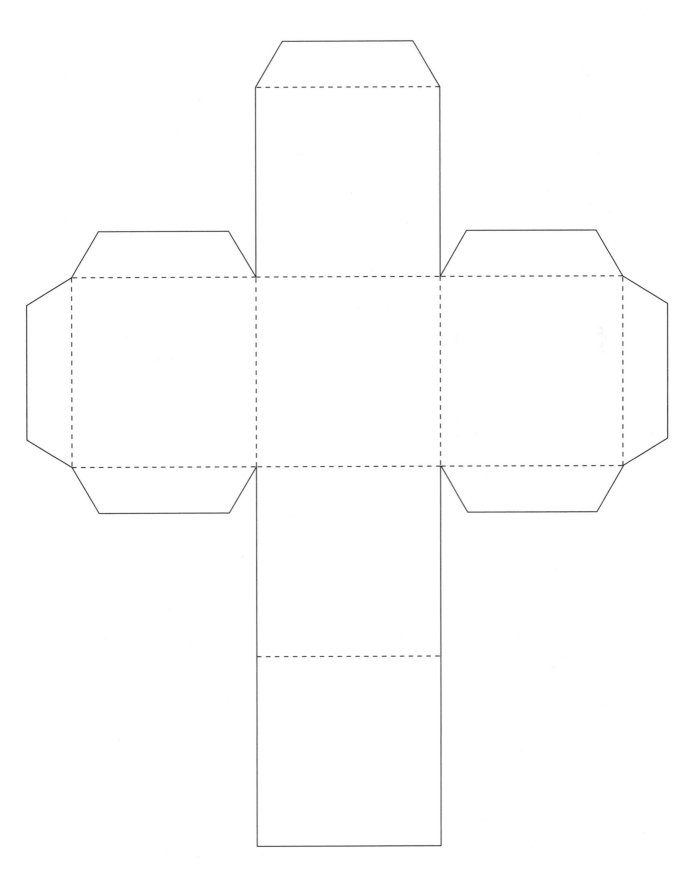

Dialogue Duets

After reading a story, invite two students to become the main characters. Provide time for the students to prepare their dialogue. The dialogue should reflect the main ideas of the story. Have the pair share the story orally in front of the class.

Diary Entries

All students enjoy being the main character in a favorite story. Model a "Dear Diary" entry on an overhead, a chalkboard, or a chart. Each child can write an entry as if he or she were that character. Illustrations may be added or substituted depending on the ability levels.

School-Home CONNECTION

Ask children to have their families prepare a diary entry describing their favorite family experience. Children may illustrate the diary entry. These entries should be returned to school for sharing. You may want to compile the entries in a large family-diary class book.

AaBbCcDdEeFfGgHhIiJjKkLlMmNnOoPpQqRrSsTtUuVvWwXxYyZz

Events to Remember

After reading a story, provide children with a white sheet of paper and instruct them to fold it into four boxes. Lead a class discussion on the different events that took place in the story. These can be listed on chart paper or on the chalkboard. Have children select four events and illustrate one in each of the four boxes.

Envelopes

Provide each student with an envelope, a one-foot length of yarn, and three index cards. Students are then invited to illustrate the beginning, middle, and end of a story on each of the index cards. Help them to punch holes in the cards and string them along the yarn. Students can then place the cards and yarn in the envelopes. They can take turns retelling their stories to each other.

School-Home CONNECTION

Invite students to take their envelopes home to retell the story to their families.

Flap Books

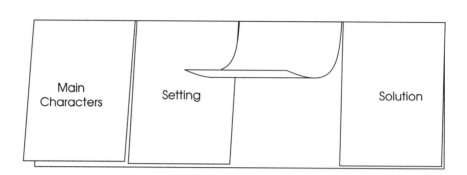

This activity works well for both fiction and nonfiction books. After reading a nonfiction book, give students a 12" x 18" sheet of white paper. Ask them to fold the paper in half lengthwise and then fold it into fourths. Then have children open up the paper and cut along each short fold on one side only, being careful to stop at the original center fold line. (See the diagram.) Each student will then have a long book with four flaps. Have students write four facts from the story on each of the flaps and illustrate them on the inside. These facts may be brainstormed together as a class and written on a chalkboard or chart paper for copying. For fiction books, ask students to label each flap with these headings: "Main Characters," "Setting," "Problem," and "Solution." Have students illustrate each of these story components. More able students may write a sentence describing what they draw.

Favorite Book Celebrations

Tell students you are going to have "Favorite Book Celebration." You might want to make this a week-long event and set aside time each day for student sharing. Invite students to select a favorite book. Ask them to take turns reading the book or a section of the book aloud. Then have them explain why the book they chose is their favorite. Create a celebration banner using computer paper that lists your students' names and the books they've chosen.

School-Home CONNECTION

Provide children with white paper to make flap books with their families. Suggested topics might include: What My Family Does For Fun, Funny Facts About My Family, or Family Favorites.

Graph It!

After reading a piece of literature in which there are several characters, ask students to voice their opinion about their favorite character or the one that is most like them. Provide each child with a self-stick note on which to draw or name the character he or she has chosen. Then have each child place the note on the appropriate place on a graph you've drawn on the chalkboard or on chart paper. (See the photo below.)

Geography Places

This project is great for collaborative groups of four to six children. After reading a book or several books that include geography terms, guide students in creating their own perfect places on large pieces of white butcher paper. Suggest that groups use at least one geography term, and include examples of proper clothing,

food, and special events in their illustrations if desired. Groups can share their completed projects with the entire class. These examples of "perfect places" may be visited as they are displayed around the classroom.

School-Home CONNECTION

Encourage families to draw and write about a dream vacation spot. These drawings can be returned to school and categorized according to location, such as beach, mountains, desert, etc. The results can be graphed and displayed in the classroom.

Hanging Mobiles

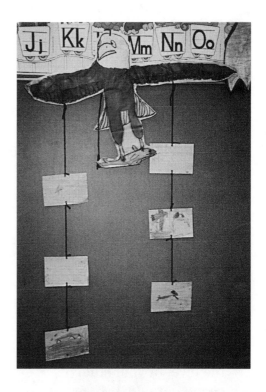

This activity is perfect to use after you've read a science book. Divide the class into collaborative groups of four to six children. Provide each group with four to six medium-sized index cards and a length of yarn. On the cards children will write and illustrate facts from the science story. After the cards are completed, students can paint a large picture to illustrate the main concept. These may be doubled, stuffed, and then stapled together to achieve a 3-D effect. The fact cards can be hung with yarn from the large painting. Add another length of yarn to the painting and hang the mobile for all to enjoy.

Hot Seat

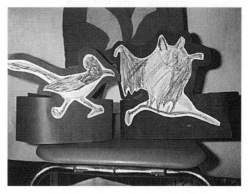

After reading a favorite story, give children the opportunity to become one of the characters by occupying the "hot seat." Have other students ask them questions about their actions in the story. You may want to decorate the hot seat with flames made out of red, orange, and yellow construction paper.

School-Home CONNECTION

Invite children and their families to make "Family Mobiles." Provide families with a large sheet of white construction paper on which to draw their home. Also send home yarn and index cards on which they can draw each member of their family, including pets. The families may wish to include information about themselves on their cards. The mobiles can be returned to school for display on back-to-school night or at an open house.

Interviews

Have students take turns playing reporter. Invite them to make up questions about a book or books you've read in class and to take turns asking each other the questions. Be sure to model some good questions for them.

Ice Cream Cones

Dip into your favorite story elements using the reproducible of the ice cream scoops provided on page 22. Depending on the level of your students, scoop out one, two, or three "flavors" to each student. Three "flavors" might represent the beginning, middle, and end of the story; two might represent a problem and solution; or one scoop might represent a favorite part of a story. Encourage students to cut out and glue their scoop(s) on top of triangular pieces of paper on which they have written the title of their story. These cones may be displayed on a bulletin board titled: "We All Scream for Ice Cream."

Interesting Incidents

Become detectives and dive into the interesting incidents found in stories you have read to your class. This activity works well when you want to review a collection of stories you have been reading, such as fairy tales, a series of books by a favorite author, or if you have several small groups reading several different stories. Encourage each group to comb through its book filing a report on the story events, such as what happened first, next, last, or on problems and solutions. These events may be written and/or illustrated on the outline of the magnifying glass on page 23. Provide time for each detective group to share its evidence. No book will go uncovered after this activity!

I.C.E. (Incidents, Characters, and Events)

There will be a chill in the air when your class participates in a game called I.C.E. After reading a story, divide your class into three teams called the "incidents," the "characters," and the "events." This game may be played in two ways. One way to play is to set your timer for three minutes and during that set time have each team work together to discuss how it will act out its story element to the class. Another way to play is to ignore the set time and provide each team with a large piece of poster paper so that it can illustrate and write about its story element. Either way, the game concludes with the sharing of a skit or drawing. The winners can be the team that worked most cooperatively, the team that worked quietly, or the team that gave the best presentation. Everyone is a winner when you play I.C.E.

School-Home CONNECTION

Provide a copy of the reproducible of the ice cream scoops for each child to take home. Encourage students to fill in their scoop with the title of their family's favorite book or their family's favorite author and the titles of his or her books they have enjoyed. These may be shared the following day with a real scoop of ice cream. Everyone will truly yell, "We All Scream for Ice Cream."

Ice Cream Cones

Interesting Incidents

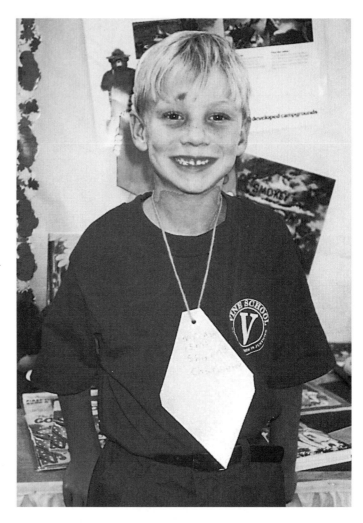

Jammin' Jewels

Students will sparkle and shine as they wear their own Jammin' Jewel necklace. After reading a piece of literature, provide each child with the outline of the "jewel" on page 25. On the jewel have students draw or write four things that really made the story shine for them. Have them cut out the jewel and string it on yarn so they can wear it around their necks. The sharing of these jewels will bring a sparkle to your day.

Jumbo Trading Cards

Invite your students to make "Jumbo Character Trading Cards" of their favorite characters using the reproducibles on pages 26-27. You may want to have students bring in baseball cards or other collectible cards before doing this activity. Make a double-sided photocopy of the reproducibles, being careful that the front and back of the copied pages align with each other. Have them draw a large picture of the character and the character's name on the front of the "card," and then complete the back. Encourage students to trade cards with one another and tell about their characters.

School-Home CONNECTION

Provide children with a jewel outline to take home. Have them tell about a favorite story by filling in the jewel with their families.

Jammin' Jewel

Character Trading Card

Character's name: _____

From the book: _____

By: _____

Other books with this character:

_____

_____

Why I like this character:

_____

_____

_____

_____

_____

Kickin' Kangaroos

Kickin' Kangaroos hold a pouch full of knowledge. Provide each child with the outline of the kangaroo on page 29 and a brown paper lunch bag that has been cut in half. The bottom half of the lunch bag will be used as the kangaroo's pouch. After coloring and cutting out the kangaroo, have students glue the pouch onto the front of the kangaroo. Provide each child with several 5" x 8" index cards on which he or she can write or illustrate the parts of the story that they got a "kick" out of. Have children take turns sharing their kangaroos.

Knowledge Charts

Knowledge charts help children take charge of their learning. Before beginning a book, set up a chart with three columns. Label the first column "What I Know," the second, "What I Want to Learn," and the third, "What I Learned." Complete the first two columns before reading a book, and the last when you've finished.

School-Home CONNECTION

Encourage children to share with their families four things that they have learned from a book they've read together at home. The poetry frame on page 30 may be used as a springboard for this home connection.

Kickin' Kangaroo

In the Know

The _____ Family Is "In The Know."

We read _____.

We know _____.

We know _____.

We know _____.

We know _____.

Our family is in the know!

AaBbCcDdEeFfGgHhIiJjKkLlMmNnOoPpQqRrSsTtUuVvWwXxYyZz

Letters

Letters to the characters in a story are an excellent way to assess children's understanding of a story. Depending upon the age and ability level of your children, you may wish to compose a class letter or have children write letters. For kindergartners you may write one simple class letter for children to copy and illustrate. First graders might add one sentence of their own to the class letter. Second graders may wish to write their own letters after a class discussion about the information or questions that the letter could contain.

Leapin' Ladders

Use copies of the reproducible on page 32 to create Leapin' Ladders. These graphic organizers can be used after reading to sequence the main events in a story. Each main event is filled in on the appropriate rung or drawn in the area between the rungs. The main characters are drawn on 3" x 5" index cards and then are cut out. Students make the characters leap up the ladder as the story is retold.

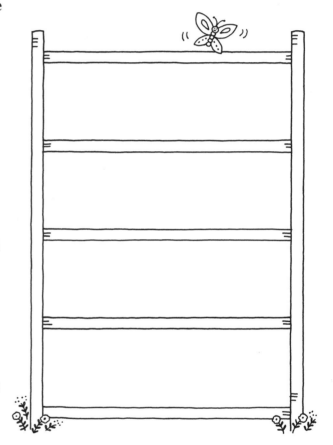

School-Home CONNECTION

Children may take home their Leapin' Ladder to share it with their families. The families can then write a letter to the class expressing their reactions to the story. After sharing the letters with the class, you may wish to bind them into a class book for display at an open house.

Name_____

Leapin' Ladder

Last:

Then:

Next:

First:

AaBbCcDdEeFfGgHhIiJjKkLlMmNnOoPpQqRrSsTtUuVvWwXxYyZz

Memory Books

Creating memory books can be a wonderful way to take an adventure with a character to new heights. A memory book is similar to a baby book, in that it represents the important events in the life of a character. Pages may include student-created pictures of the character, as well as small artifacts that represent important milestones in the life of the character. For example, a piece of the fabric woven by Christopher Columbus in his father's weaving shop, a map handmade by Columbus, or a picture of his first ship might be included as artifacts.

This literature activity is best completed in collaborative groups of three to five children. You may wish to assign each group a different character, fictional or nonfictional. Completed books should be shared with the whole class, thereby exposing the class to a number of different characters.

Matrixes

A matrix is a pictorial representation of several books that have been read on the same theme which share the same story elements. Divide your class into groups of five and assign each group a different book. Each member of the group is responsible for the illustration of one of these story elements: title and author, main characters, setting, problem, and solution. You may wish to have students use 5" x 8" index cards for their illustrations. Cut a piece of butcher paper large enough to display all the index cards. Divide the butcher paper into five sections and label each of the five story elements across the top. Invite students to glue the completed index cards onto the butcher paper horizontally according to the title and story elements. Display and use as a tool for comparing the many stories.

AaBbCcDdEeFfGgHhIiJjKkLlMmNnOoPpQqRrSsTtUuVvWwXxYyZz

Movie Posters

Lights! Camera! Action! Encourage children to work in groups turning their favorite book into "movies." Have them spotlight the "movies" by creating colorful posters advertising the upcoming event—the event being the acting out of the book by the children. Posters should include: title, author, and a scene from the "movie." You might even capture the fun on video tape. Quiet on the set!

School-Home CONNECTION

Supply children with several sheets of drawing paper and invite them to create a family memory book based on a family celebration or special event. Encourage the inclusion of illustrations or small artifacts that depict the special occasion. These memory books can be shared and displayed at school.

Notepads

Share examples of character notepads with the class which reflect the main characters in a story and their interests. For example, a notepad for *Jack and the Beanstalk*, might be designed with a border of vines, golden eggs, or both. To make notepads, provide children with pieces of 4" x 6" paper that they can staple together at the top. Depending on the level of your students, these may be shared and used by other students to write notes as if they are that character.

Necklaces

Story necklaces become the hottest fashion statement on any primary playground. After reading a story provide each child with three small index cards and a length of yarn, long enough to make a necklace. Guide children as they illustrate on each of the index cards the main characters, the problem, and the solution; or what happened first, next, and last in the story. When completed, punch a hole in each index card and have children string them onto the length of yarn. Encourage children to adorn their "jewelry" and to share them on the playground during recess or on a visit to another classroom.

Newspapers

Extra! Extra! Extra! Read all about it. Newspapers become a colorful tool to share a story or collection of stories based on a theme the class has been studying. Children may be divided into small groups and within the groups two or three children can collaborate on writing the news article, while the others prepare the illustrations. If computers are available you may wish to have children publish the final copy. Many simple computer programs are available that will set up the page in the format of a newspaper. If you do not have a computer available, children's articles and illustrations may be glued onto a large sheet of paper on which you have drawn lines for the columns and headlines.

School-Home CONNECTION

Send home instructions to families to write articles that will be compiled into a classroom family newspaper. Suggested articles might deal with topics such as parenting tips, book reviews, restaurant reviews, recipes, movie reviews, or favorite travel spots. You may assign students a topic or allow them to select one. The articles should be returned to school and compiled into a newspaper to be reproduced and sent home.

Octopuses

Using the outline of the octopus provided on page 38, invite children to draw or write on the tentacles the name of the story; the author; what happened first, next, and last; favorite part or character; and new words learned. They can write their names on the eighth tentacle. Create a sea of octopuses by hanging them from the ceiling.

One-Minute Book Talks

When time is a factor during the busy teaching day, one-minute book talks help in allowing all students to share a book they have enjoyed. Posters created by the students enhance the book talks and serve as a colorful tool as they give their reviews.

School-Home CONNECTION

One-minute book talks can be shared at home, and families may respond by writing a one-line positive comment about each child's book talk. These notes my be compiled into a booklet entitled "Positive One Liners."

Octopus

38

Postcards

After reading a story, provide students with a large index card that is lined on one side with which to make a postcard. Students' postcards may be written to a character in the story from the student, or from one character to another, or from the student to a friend telling them about the story. Be sure to have students appropriately illustrate the blank side of their cards. You may wish to show students samples of different postcards you have collected so that they might have a better understanding of the final product. Depending upon the age and ability level of your class, you may vary the writing part of the assignment from individual cards to a class-composed postcard or use a postcard frame that you have composed ahead of time.

Pop-Out Character Masks

A pop-out character mask is fun to make and use in the retelling of a story. Invite each student to select a favorite character. Provide him or her with a shallow box or lid in which you've cut a large oval that allows the child's face to show through. Features, such as hair and hats, may be drawn, colored, or added with other materials. Have children take turns telling their stories while wearing their masks.

School-Home CONNECTION

Encourage children to retell their stories at home while wearing their masks.

Quick Questions

Before reading a story ask students to make predictions about the book, based on the cover or any background information they might have about the author or subject. Record students' responses on an overhead, a chalkboard, or on chart paper for further reference. As you read the story, pause to check students' responses and model an appropriate question based on the content of the book and the predictions made. For example, before reading *Jack and the Beanstalk*, students may have predicted that the story is about a boy living a long time ago. As you read the story and notice the illustrations and the text, you can stop and ask students, "Were we correct in predicting that this story took place a long time ago?" Find support for your answer in the text or illustrations. This activity is good preparation for independent reading and comprehension. You are teaching students to check the text and illustrations for meaning.

"Queen" or "King" for the Day

Select a volunteer to be the "Queen" or "King" of the day for your class "reading court." After reading a story, the Queen or King selects the character from the story who she or he would most like to be for the day. This student is given a copy of the crown provided on page 41. After coloring and cutting out the crown, the Queen or King draws a picture of the character in the oval on the front of the crown.  Your Queen or King will proudly wear the crown in the classroom. The wearing of this crown entitles the Queen or King to special privileges throughout the day, such as being a line leader, class helper, and so on.

School-Home CONNECTION

The Queen or King of the day is encouraged to wear the crown home and retell the story to his or her home court.

Queen or King for a Day

Repeat pattern on 12" by 18" paper.

41

Rr

Report Card

Character's Name _____

Name of Book _____

Teacher's Name _____

Subject	Grade	Comments

GRADING KEY
A = Awesome
G = Good job
C = Could do better

AaBbCcDdEeFfGgHhIiJjKkLlMmNnOoPpQqRrSsTtUuVvWwXxYyZz

Report Cards

After reading a story, lead the class in preparing a "report card" for the main character. You may wish to use the form of the report card provided on page 43. Explain to the class that this report card will be different than the report card each of them receives in school. After modeling the report card, divide the class into groups of four to six students and ask them to make up their own report card for the main character. These report cards may be shared with the whole group upon completion.

Reciprocal Reading

Even non-readers can be encouraged to participate in this activity by "reading" the illustrations in a book. Students work in pairs taking turns reading a story. One child reads a page and asks questions of his or her partner. The roles are switched for the next page, and the child who was listening now becomes the reader and questioner. These roles are alternated until the book is completed or time is up.

Round Up

After studying a theme, "round up" all of the books used during the theme and pass them out to members of your class. Each student with a book is responsible for a quick-share on that book, explaining how it related to the theme, what he or she learned from the book, or what he or she liked about it. This activity is fun to do while sitting in a large circle around a "campfire." This reader round up is a nice culmination before riding off to the next theme.

School-Home CONNECTION

Encourage students to try out reciprocal reading with a family member. Students may wish to share the book they read at home and a sample question with their class.

AaBbCcDdEeFfGgHhIiJjKkLlMmNnOoPpQqRrSsTtUuVvWwXxYyZz

Report Card

Character's Name _____

Name of Book _____

Teacher's Name _____

Subject   Grade   Comments

_____   _____   _____

                                              _____

                                              _____

_____   _____   _____

                                              _____

                                              _____

_____   _____   _____

                                              _____

GRADING KEY

A = Awesome

G = Good job

C = Could do better

AaBbCcDdEeFfGgHhIiJjKkLlMmNnOoPpQqRrSsTtUuVvWwXxYyZz

Sketch It

After reading a story, divide your class into groups of four or five students. Provide each group with a large piece of white butcher paper. Encourage students to draw symbols or pictures on the butcher paper that represent events in the story. This activity lends itself to total participation from all members of the group. Completed sketches may be shared and displayed around the classroom.

Story Belts

Story belts can be constructed out of recycled tag board sentence strips or new strips can be cut from a large sheet of tag board. After reading a story, invite students to draw a story map, illustrate several story elements, or to relate what happened first, next, or last on their story belts. You may wish to have students punch holes at certain intervals along the belts and then stitch through the holes with brown yarn. The loose ends of the yarn are tied together for a perfect fit.

Shoe Stories

What child doesn't love to work with small items? Each "shoe story" is made from an unruled 3" x 5" index card that has been folded in half. These tiny books are made after a story is read and may contain pictures of certain story elements or the sequence of events in a story. They are called "shoe stories" because when they are completed, they are hole punched in the upper corner, strung with a short length of yarn, and tied onto the students' shoes. They get a wonderful reaction on the playground! Children gather excitedly around the feet of the shoe storyteller while the story is retold.

School-Home CONNECTION

Provide each student with a strip of tag board to take home. Encourage family members to create a "Super Family Story Belt" with their own illustrations or illustrations copied from a favorite family story or book. Students may wear these belts to school the next day. Good stories are a cinch with story belts!

T-Frames

T-frames are used to review the actions of a character after reading a story. Provide students with a large sheet of white paper and guide them as they fold it to create two boxes. Guide students in writing the character's name at the top of one half and their name on the other side at the top. Then have students select two incidents that involved the character and write or draw these incidents under the character's name. On the side write under their name, they should write or draw how they would react in that situation. For example, in the story *Jack and the Beanstalk*, Jack traded the cow for magic beans, but the student might have asked for beans and money. More capable students might add a written explanation to their illustrations.

Triaramas

Triaramas are a fun way to check comprehension. To make a triarama, fold a paper square diagonally one way, open it, and then fold it diagonally the other way. (See the diagram.) Open the paper out flat and cut from one corner to the mid-point. Put an "X" on one of the cut "legs" to remind students that this leg should not be drawn or written on because it will be glued under the other leg. After reading a story the students may draw or write the beginning, middle and the end of the story on their triarama. When constructed, triaramas will be 3-D. The use of this technique is unlimited.

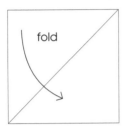

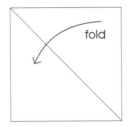

Travelin' Turtle Backpacks

Your students can travel from class to class or onto the playground toting their own "travelin' turtle backpacks." Provide small groups of students with a copy of the turtle reproducible on page 48. Have them cut out and glue the turtle onto a large paper grocery bag. Straps for these toting turtles may be added out of yarn or strips of heavy paper. Then have students work together to make puppets of characters from their favorite stories. These puppets may be glued onto tongue depressors. Students can place the puppets inside their travelin' turtle backpacks and take turns having a storytelling adventure.

School-Home CONNECTION

Encourage children to take turns wearing their travelin' turtle backpacks home to retell the story to their families. Tuck in an index card or small journal for the families to record their reactions to the storytelling.

Uu

Unique T-Shirts

"Unique T-shirts" can be created using an 8" x 8" piece of white paper and a pattern made from a small child's T-shirt. The paper square is folded to make four boxes. In the boxes students might draw a picture of themselves, write the title of their favorite book, write the author's name, and draw a character or scene from the book. Use the pattern to trace a T-shirt shape on construction paper. The completed square is glued on the T-shirt. Children can write their names in large letters above the square. For a unique bulletin board you can mount the T-shirts and add a smiling paper-plate face adorned with yarn hair to top off each T-shirt.

School-Home CONNECTION

Unique T-shirts become a family project as members create a family portrait. Family members should be encouraged to draw themselves wearing or doing something that is a clue to a favorite activity or hobby they enjoy. What a unifying experience!

Venn Diagrams

Venn diagrams can help your class compare similarities and differences in the setting, characters, or story lines of two books. They may be introduced through the use of two hula hoops or with two large rings made from yarn. You may also want to model how to use

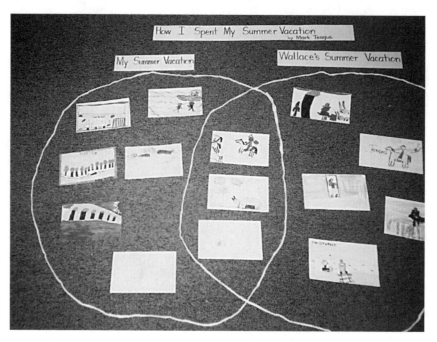

Venn diagrams on the overhead or on the chalkboard. This activity lends itself nicely to small group work.

Visors

Provide each child with the outline of the visor on page 52. Students may design a visor for the main character of a story they have recently read. The visor would reflect interests or incidents from the main character's life. More capable students can include

a written explanation of their illustrations. After the visors have been colored, invite students to cut them out, attach yarn, and wear them while sharing their thoughts about the story.

Visual Synthesis

This activity is best used following a book that has a moral or a specific life lesson to be learned. After reading, assist students in selecting a sentence from the story that best summarizes the theme. Provide large pieces of butcher paper for small groups of students to illustrate the sentence selected. Make sure they include their sentences with their illustrations.

School-Home CONNECTION

Provide students with a copy of the visor to take home to make a visual synthesis visor. This visor can be completed at home after a favorite book is read.

Visor

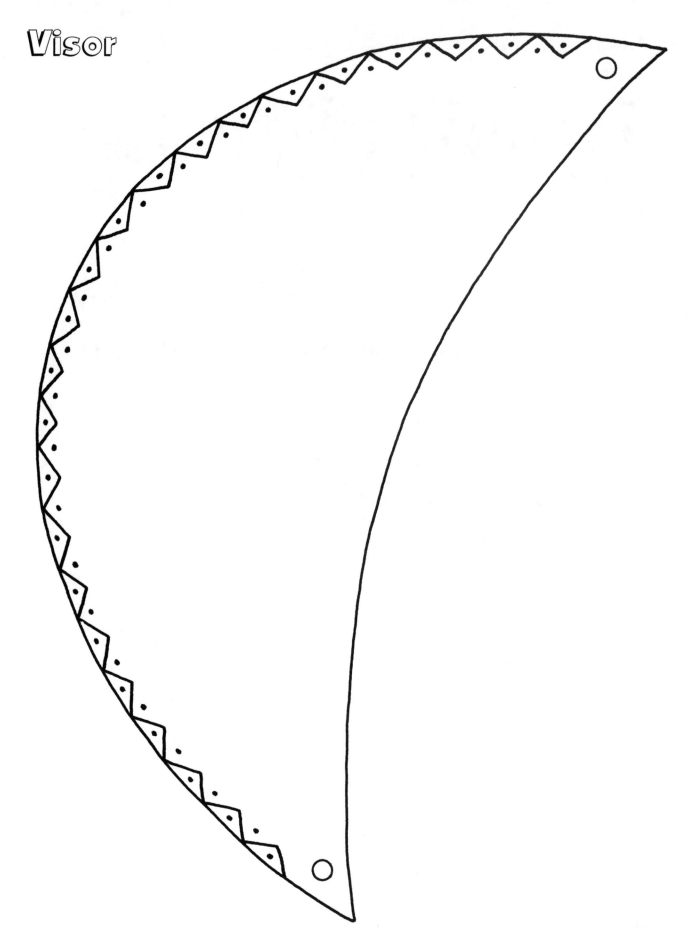

Wanted Posters

Wanted posters can be created from a large sheet of white construction paper. The top half of the paper is used to draw a picture of the "wanted" character while the bottom half contains information about that character such as a physical description and his or her habits and interests. Symbols may also be drawn to represent the character. It is best to first model this literature extension with the whole class before asking them to do it. Don't forget to offer an appropriate reward.

Word Problems

Word problems can be created for many stories to make a math link. This activity should be modeled as a whole-class activity first. After reading a story, divide the class into small groups of four to six students and assign each group a math concept to use in writing its word problems. Remind students to use information from the story in the math word problem and to include the answer. Illustrations add greatly to the assignment and aid in explaining the word problems.

Wonderful Whales

What child doesn't fall in love with our gentle whale friends? After reading a book, provide children with the outline of the whale provided on page 54. On the outline children may tell what was wonderful in the story they have just read. This is a whale of a way to share what students liked about the book.

School-Home CONNECTION

Provide copies of the whale outline for students to take home to complete with their families about a favorite book.

Wonderful Whale

X-ray Those Bones!

Take an "inside" view of a story using the outlines of the bones on pages 56–58. This is an eXcellent activity for all ages.

Stories with a humorous slant certainly lend themselves to the use of the "funny" bone. Instruct students to select the part of the story that was funniest to them and to draw a picture describing it on the funny bone. Students with more ability may also add a written explanation. This is guaranteed to tickle the whole class.

Stories of a more serious nature are best illustrated or described on the outline of the backbone. Students may draw what they feel was the main point of the story. This bone can also be used to illustrate the strengths of the main character or what students learned from the story.

Stories with a more wistful, dream-like quality would best be illustrated or described on the outline provided of the wishbone. Students may either draw the main character's wish or a wish of their own. This activity may be used across the curriculum.

Completed bones should be cut out, strung together on a length of string or yarn, and hung from the ceiling or a clothesline.

School-Home CONNECTION

Any of the bone outlines may be copied and sent home. Families may fill out the bone that relates to a favorite story they have read at home during that week.

Funny Bone

Back Bone

Wish Bone

"You Defend the Character" Headbands

After reading, students select or are assigned a character in the story to defend. They make a headband using the outline on page 60 to identify which character they are portraying. Other students work in small groups creating questions they would like to ask the character. When they have prepared their questions, the character is invited to sit at the front of the classroom and the class proceeds to ask questions of this character. The character responds based on the events in the story and according to his or her knowledge. This activity should be modeled before students work on their own.

School-Home CONNECTION

Students may take home the character headbands and tell their families the story from that character's point of view. Encourage families to ask questions of the character and about the character's actions in the story.

"You Defend the Character" Headband

MY Character

Zz

Zoom In

Focus on one aspect of a story such as character development, plot, or problem and solution. Provide students with copies of the outline of the camera provided on page 62. Encourage them to color and cut out the camera. On the back, have students draw or write a story element of your choice. Attach a piece of yarn to the camera so that students can hang them around their necks. Smile, say "cheese," and share.

Zip It Up

To practice making predictions and increase active participation while reading, try "Zip It Up" with your class. You can use the outline of the zipper on page 63 as an overhead or make it into a large chart. As you read a story aloud, stop after every couple of pages, asking the students what they think will happen next. Record the students' predictions on either side of the zipper (one prediction on one side, alternate to the opposite side of the zipper for the next prediction). You may continue this throughout the reading of the story, always stopping at a part of the story which lends itself to good predictions.

When you are finished reading the story and making predictions, review the predictions and make note of those that were accurate by highlighting or circling them. The actual events of the story can be written up in the space in the middle of the zipper. Zip up your story by reviewing the predictions made and how they compare to the actual events of the story.

School-Home CONNECTION

Have students bring the camera outline home and complete it with their families after reading a favorite book.

Zoom In

Notes

_____

_____

_____

_____

_____

_____

_____

_____

_____

_____

_____

_____

AaBbCcDdEeFfGgHhIiJjKkLlMmNnOoPpQqRrSsTtUuVvWwXxYyZz